This book belongs to ....

I am .... (Age)

People sometimes call me ....

.... (My Nickname)

I live at ....

3

The Big Picture!

Have you ever tried one of those large, complicated jigsaw puzzles? Each individual piece fits somewhere, but at first you have no idea where! When it's done, however, it's no longer a puzzle and all the clues are obvious.

Our life's journey is like part of a jigsaw puzzle. Each one of us owns a piece of this Mega Jigsaw Puzzle of life, but we can't yet see where our piece fits. Only God knows the Big Picture. The Bible tells us about the life journeys of many people and we can see how their piece of the puzzle fits into God's overall plan. Through this series of 60 readings, even young children can explore the lives of some of these people. Their stories are part of a series of Hotshots books, written at the child's level of understanding and enjoyment. The relevant Bible passages are included, quoted from the *Contemporary English Version,* which is available from the Bible Society and widely recommended for children and adults alike.

The children will be able to explore how the lives of some of the characters in the Bible relate to their own. As they get to know these Bible characters and how their lives fit into God's Mega Jigsaw Puzzle, the children will discover that they themselves are part of the Big Picture too.

Hotshots contains things to think about, and projects to do either individually or as part of a family. Your child may need your support and encouragement to complete some of the activities.

We pray that as children discover the stories in the Bible they will learn to love the One who sees the Big Picture. We also pray that they will become aware that they have an important part to play in the Big Picture of God who loves them dearly.

Getting Started with  hotshots

The Bible is full of stories about people. This *Hotshots* will introduce you to four of these people.

Choose when and where to do your *Hotshots* readings.

My decision:

The best time for me to read *Hotshots* is

_____ (when)

I will record important things

_____ (where)

Imagine what i

...travel back through time

That's exactly what the people in this book do.

Meet **Captain Kate** and her crew. They call themselves the **Hotshots**. Every Wednesday after school the Hotshots meet in their Clubhouse in Kate's backyard. Kate is Captain so she has an important job to do. But so do the other Hotshots.

Normal Kate...

Hi! I'm Reuben. I'm in charge of maintenance – like painting the Time-ship name!.

I'm Alana. I check the instruments, and tune the electronics.

My name is Suzy. I look after the fuel supply.

ould be like to...

ee people who lived long ago.

The Hotshots are planning to check out four people who lived a long time ago: Abraham, Jonah, Peter and Paul.

Would you like to come? Then ... Climb aboard...

My name's Mei. I'm in charge of research.

... Captain Kate!

I'm Sean. My job is to keep the maps in order.

Oops!!! One thing first...

How do the Hotsho
people they ar

Kate told them.
She read the
true stories
of ...

Peter

Jonah

Abraham

Paul

... in her Bible.

This Hotshots book includes
the parts of the Bible you will
need to read about them too.
They are next to this symbol.

nOw about the
oing to viSit?

If you need to look up things in your Bible, here's how ... Each verse has a REFERENCE. It's a bit like an address. It tells you where to find the verse. This is what a reference looks like.

Genesis 12: 1-5

The book of the Bible	Chapter 12	Verses 1 to 5

1 Find the book you need in the contents page of your Bible. (There are 66 books in a full Bible.) Look at the page number and turn to that page.

2 Find the chapter by looking at the big numbers on the page or the heading at the top.

3 Find the verse by looking at the little numbers in the chapter.

ow this book to your parents. You could ask them to help you with some of it.

NOw, climb aboard ... and off we go!

Starting an adventure

Genesis 12:1-5

The Lord said to Abram:

Leave your country, your family, and your relatives and go to the land that I will show you. ² I will bless you and make your descendants into a great nation. You will become famous and be a blessing to others. ³ I will bless anyone who blesses you, but I will put a curse on anyone who puts a curse on you. Everyone on earth will be blessed because of you.

4-5 Abram was seventy-five years old when the Lord told him to leave the city of Haran. He obeyed and left with his wife Sarai, his nephew Lot, and all the possessions and slaves they had gotten while in Haran.

Have you ever moved with your family to a place where you knew no one?

God told Abram to leave his country and go to a place he had never seen.

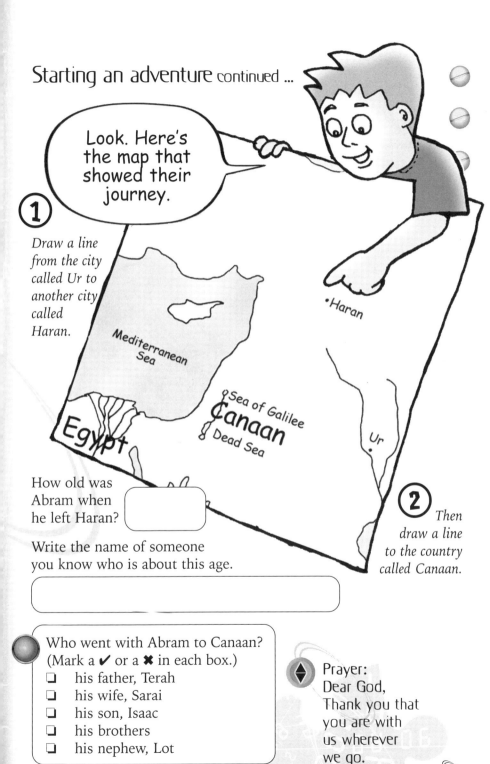

Look. Here's the map that showed their journey.

1

Draw a line from the city called Ur to another city called Haran.

•Haran

Mediterranean Sea

Egypt

Sea of Galilee

Canaan

Dead Sea

Ur

How old was Abram when he left Haran?

Write the name of someone you know who is about this age.

2 Then draw a line to the country called Canaan.

Who went with Abram to Canaan?
(Mark a ✔ or a ✖ in each box.)
❑ his father, Terah
❑ his wife, Sarai
❑ his son, Isaac
❑ his brothers
❑ his nephew, Lot

Prayer:
Dear God,
Thank you that you are with us wherever we go.

A special promise

Look! The new skateboard mum and dad promised me.

Sean was so excited. His parents had promised to give him a new skate board for Christmas. How do you think he felt?

God promised Abram something very special. See if you can find God's promise in the Bible passage. Underline it with a green pencil.

Genesis 12:6-9

⁶ Abram went as far as the sacred tree of Moreh in a place called Shechem. The Canaanites were still living in the land at that time, ⁷ but the Lord appeared to Abram and promised, "I will give this land to your family forever." Abram then built an altar there for the Lord.

⁸ Abram travelled to the hill country east of Bethel and camped between Bethel and Ai, where he built another altar and worshiped the Lord. ⁹ Later, Abram started out toward the Southern Desert.

God always keeps His promises. Abram's great, great, great, great, great, great ......grandchildren still live in that land today. Now it's in the country called Israel.

Prayer:
Thank you God that you always keep your promises.

Mei's
Research Page

Abraham

Where did Abram come from?

Abram came from a city called Ur.

Ur was once one of the oldest and most important cities. Archaeologists digging in the ruins found writing on blocks of clay. They call them 'tablets'. They tell about the people who lived there. They discovered ancient tombs, full of gold and silver.

People lived in two storey houses. They had schools in Ur.

What was the religion in Ur?

Ur had a large building for the moon god, Nanna. It was built in three stages, with a temple to Nanna on the top. The temple had a long central staircase and two other staircases. Smaller staircases led up to the temple.

When did he find out about the true God?

No one knows. But we do know that Abram responded when God spoke to him.

What do we know about Abram at this time?

Abram was an adventurous person. He was 75 years old when God told him to pack up and go to another country. He obeyed God even though he didn't know where God was leading him. For the rest of his life he would live in a tent and move from place to place.

IMPORTANT!

Abram trusted God. God gave him a special promise.
He believed that God would keep his word.

Here's trouble

I want it. I want to have a go.

No! This belongs to me. You can't have it.

Did you know the Bible records some arguments?

Genesis 13:1-7

Abram and Sarai took everything they owned and went to the Southern Desert. Lot went with them.

² Abram was very rich. He owned many cattle, sheep, and goats, and had a lot of silver and gold. ³ Abram moved from place to place in the Southern Desert. And finally, he went north and set up his tents between Bethel and Ai, ⁴ where he had earlier camped and built an altar. There he worshiped the Lord.

⁵ Lot, who was travelling with him, also had sheep, goats, and cattle, as well as his own family and slaves. ⁶⁻⁷ At this time the Canaanites and the Perizzites were living in the same area, and so there wasn't enough pastureland left for Abram and Lot with all of their animals. Besides this, the men who took care of Abram's animals and the ones who took care of Lot's animals started quarrelling.

Find some good advice about arguing in Proverbs 14:29 in your Bible.

Write the verse in the frame.

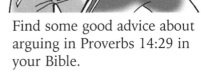

It is easy to argue. It is much more difficult to stop and think first.

Prayer:
Dear God, help me not to argue, but to stop and think first.

What I really want

The Hotshots were planning their trip in the Time Machine. Suzy's mother had made them all some little cakes. Suzy passed the plate of cakes to Mei. One of the cakes was much larger than the others.

Which cake would you choose? Draw a red circle around it.

Genesis 13:8-13

[8] Abram said to Lot, "We are close relatives. We shouldn't argue, and our men shouldn't be fighting one another. [9] There is plenty of land for you to choose from. Let's separate. If you go north, I'll go south; if you go south, I'll go north."

[10] This happened before the Lord had destroyed the cities of Sodom and Gomorrah. And when Lot looked around, he saw there was plenty of water in the Jordan Valley. All the way to Zoar the valley was as green as the garden of the Lord or the land of Egypt. [11] So Lot chose the whole Jordan Valley for himself, and as he started toward the east, he and Abram separated. [12] Abram stayed in the land of Canaan. But Lot settled near the cities of the valley and put up his tents not far from Sodom, [13] where the people were evil and sinned terribly against the Lord.

Who chose the best land?

Draw a red circle around his name in the reading.

Lot was selfish but Abram was

_ _ selfish.

(Finish the word.)

 Prayer:
Dear God, please help me not to be selfish, but to be happy to share.

5

Another promise

Genesis 15:1-6

Later the Lord spoke to Abram in a vision, "Abram, don't be afraid! I will protect you and reward you greatly."

² But Abram answered, "Lord All-Powerful, you have given me everything I could ask for, except children. And when I die, Eliezer of Damascus will get all I own. ³ You have not given me any children, and this servant of mine will inherit everything."

⁴ The Lord replied, "No, he won't! You will have a son of your own, and everything you have will be his." ⁵ Then the Lord took Abram outside and said, "Look at the sky and see if you can count the stars. That's how many descendants you will have." ⁶ Abram believed the Lord, and the Lord was pleased with him.

Find the promise that God made to Abram. Underline it with a green pencil.

What did God tell Abram to count? Why?

Descendants are children, grandchildren and their children. How many descendants does your Grandmother have?

Something to do

Ask your mum or dad to help you work out how many descendants *their* grandparents have.

Prayer:
Dear God, Thank you that we can be part of Your family.

A look into the future

Remember the special promise God gave to Abram? Abram would be glad to know he was going to have lots of descendants but there was a sad part to the promise too.

Genesis 15:12-15

12 As the sun was setting, Abram fell into a deep sleep, and everything became dark and frightening. 13 Then the Lord said:

Abram, you will live to an old age and die in peace.

But I solemnly promise that your descendants will live as foreigners in a land that doesn't belong to them. They will be forced into slavery and abused for four hundred years. But I will terribly punish the nation that enslaves them, and they will leave with many possessions.

What would happen to Abram's descendants?

Underline the answer in red.

Prayer:
Dear God, You know everything before it happens. Help me to trust You.

Can you read the hidden message?

GodKnowSevErYthiNgeVenbefoReItHaPPEnS

Names & Meanings

Mei gave me this great book. It tells what your name means.

What your name means...

Here's some of the Hotshots' names with their meanings.

Suzy: Trusting.

Alana: Good looking and fair.

Reuben: Good son.

Write your name here. Ask someone to help you find its meaning.

Name

_____

Meaning

_____

_____

What's in a name?

Underline the names in this Bible reading.

Genesis 17:1-8

Abram was ninety-nine years old when the Lord appeared to him again and said, "I am God All-Powerful. If you obey me and always do right, ² I will keep my solemn promise to you and give you more descendants than can be counted." ³ Abram bowed with his face to the ground, and God said:

⁴ I promise that you will be the father of many nations. That's why I now change your name from Abram to Abraham. ⁶ I will give you a lot of descendants, and in the future they will become great nations. Some of them will even be kings.

⁷ I will always keep the promise I have made to you and your descendants, because I am your God and their God. ⁸ I will give you and them the land in which you are now a foreigner. I will give the whole land of Canaan to your family forever, and I will be their God.

What name did God call Himself in verse 1?

```
_____

_____
```

What new name did God give Abram?

```
_____
```

(This name means FATHER OF MANY.)

God also promised Abram a land of his own.
❏ *Tick when you've underlined this promise in verse 8.* But best of all, God promised to be their God.

Prayer Idea:
God is good to his people. Think of some of the good things God does for you, then say a thankyou prayer.

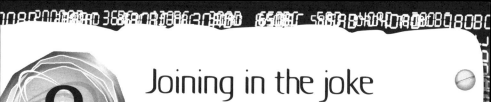

8 Joining in the joke

You might be able to hear God talking with Abraham. Read what was said …

TIME TRAVEL ALERT!

[15] Abraham, your wife's name will now be Sarah instead of Sarai. [16] I will bless her, and you will have a son by her. She will become the mother of nations, and some of her descendants will even be kings.

[17] Abraham bowed with his face to the ground and thought, "I am almost a hundred years old. How can I become a father? And Sarah is ninety. How can she have a child?" So he started laughing. [18] Then he asked God, "Why not let Ishmael inherit what you have promised me?"

[19] But God answered:
No! You and Sarah will have a son. His name will be Isaac, and I will make an everlasting promise to him and his descendants.

Continued over page

Joining in the joke continued ...

Did you hear that? God gave Abraham's wife a new name too.

Yes, and a promise as well. But do you see how old she is? She can't have a baby.

I wouldn't be so sure about that. When God makes a promise, he keeps it.

Here are some promises God has made to those who love him.

Write the baby's name in the box.

This name in Abraham's language sounds like 'laugh'.

Circle the one you like best.
Underline any you sometimes forget.

Obey me and I will be your God.

I will be with you wherever you go.

You'll find me when you search for me with all your heart.

One day everyone will know I am God.

In heaven there will be no death or pain.

Prayer idea:
Isn't it good to have the Bible and God's Spirit to tell us that God loves us? You might like to pray, thanking God for these.

9

Thought we'd drop in

Genesis 18:1-8

One hot summer afternoon Abraham was sitting by the entrance to his tent near the sacred trees of Mamre, when the Lord appeared to him. ² Abraham looked up and saw three men standing nearby. He quickly ran to meet them, bowed with his face to the ground, ³ and said, "Please come to my home where I can serve you. ⁴ I'll have some water brought, so you can wash your feet, then you can rest under the tree. ⁵ Let me get you some food to give you strength before you leave. I would be honoured to serve you."

"Thank you very much," they answered. "We accept your offer."

⁶ Abraham quickly went to his tent and said to Sarah, "Hurry! Get a large sack of flour and make some bread." ⁷ After saying this, he rushed off to his herd of cattle and picked out one of the best calves, which his servant quickly prepared. ⁸ He then served his guests some yoghurt and milk together with the meat.

People did things differently long ago. See what they did when visitors dropped by.

What do you do when visitors come to your place? ✔ those you do.

☐ wash their feet
☐ bring them food
☐ show them where to sit
☐ talk with them

Draw your favourite meal.

Prayer:
Dear God, please help me to be helpful when visitors come.

Believe it or not!

The Hotshots stood and watched Abraham and his visitors in the distance. You can read what they saw happen.

Genesis 18:9-14

While they were eating, he stood near them under the trees.⁹ and they asked, "Where is your wife Sarah?"

"She is right there in the tent," Abraham answered.

¹⁰ One of the guests was the Lord, and he said, "I'll come back about this time next year, and when I do, Sarah will already have a son."

Sarah was behind Abraham, listening at the entrance to the tent. ¹¹ Abraham and Sarah were very old, and Sarah was well past the age for having children. ¹² So she laughed and said to herself, "Now that I am worn out and my husband is old, will I really know such happiness?"

¹³ The Lord asked Abraham, "Why did Sarah laugh? Does she doubt that she can have a child in her old age? ¹⁴ I am the Lord! There is nothing too difficult for me. I'll come back next year at the time I promised, and Sarah will already have a son."

I wonder if Abraham and Sarah know who their special visitors are?

What did the Lord say to Abraham in verse 14?
Write the first 7 words on the lines.

_____

_____

_____

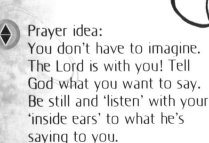

Imagine if the Lord came to your home. Do you think you'd know who it was?

What would you say?

What do you think the Lord would say to you?

Prayer idea:
You don't have to imagine. The Lord is with you! Tell God what you want to say. Be still and 'listen' with your 'inside ears' to what he's saying to you.

TO the time-ship everyone! Back to the 21st century...

A promise kept

The adventure was over and the Hotshots were back in their clubhouse.

I wish we didn't have to come back so soon.

Now we'll never know if Abraham and Sarah had that baby.

Yes we will! It's in the Bible. Let's check it out.

Genesis 21:1-6

The Lord was good to Sarah and kept his promise. ² Although Abraham was very old, Sarah had a son exactly at the time God had said. ³ Abraham named his son Isaac, ⁴ and when the boy was eight days old, Abraham circumcised him, just as the Lord had commanded.

⁵ Abraham was a hundred years old when Isaac was born, ⁶ and Sarah said, "God has made me laugh. Now everyone will laugh with me.

Here's what Kate told the Hotshots after they read the Bible.

_____

_____

Prayer:
Thank you God that you always keep your promises.
Please help me to be truthful like you.

hotshots

help *you* to read and understand the Bible

The first four books are about a Basketball Club:

- The World's Greatest Leader – ever!
- Mini-Stars of the Bible
- Growing as a Follower of Jesus
- Sticking Close to God

HOT new series

Then there are more Hotshots books ...

These books feature a new Kids' Club, their leader Kate, and their very own Time Machine!

Keep reading the Hotshots series – they will help you read the Bible.

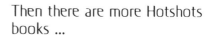

A change of plan

Kate! Come and see this. I think I've got Isaac. Isn't he growing up fast? But who's that playing beside him?

Suzy is in the time-ship. She has a screen that tunes in to other times.

Genesis 21:8-14

8 The time came when Sarah no longer had to nurse Isaac, and on that day Abraham gave a big feast.

9 One day, Sarah noticed Hagar's son Ishmael playing, and she said to Abraham, "Get rid of that Egyptian slave woman and her son! I don't want him to inherit anything. It should all go to my son."

11 Abraham was worried about Ishmael. 12 But God said, "Abraham, don't worry about your slave woman and the boy. Just do what Sarah tells you. Isaac will inherit your family name, 13 but the son of the slave woman is also your son, and I will make his descendants into a great nation."

14 Early the next morning Abraham gave Hagar an animal skin full of water and some bread. Then he put the boy on her shoulder and sent them away.

That will be Ishmael, Isaac's older stepbrother. The Bible can tell us more about him.

Join Ishmael and Isaac to their correct parents.

Sarah

Abraham

Hagar

Isaac

Ishmael

Sarah was jealous of Ishmael, wasn't she?

She didn't want him to be more important than Isaac.

Prayer:
Dear God, help us to remember that many children have no home at all. Please care for them in a special way.

Mei's
Research Page

We didn't see any babies when we time travelled to see Abraham but I've discovered some information about them.

Babies in Bible times

Baby boys were *circumcised* when they were eight days old. That means they had some skin cut off in a very small operation. It was a sign that they were one of God's people.

Hebrew mothers nursed their babies until they were about three years old. After that they were weaned. (That means the baby didn't drink milk from its mother any more.)

Weaning was the time for a party!

Cool water

13

Did Abraham really send Hagar and her son into the desert?

Let's see. We'll read about it on the way.

All aboard the time-ship!

Genesis 21:14b-16

They wandered around in the desert near Beersheba, [15] and after they had run out of water, Hagar put her son under a bush. [16] Then she sat down a long way off, because she could not bear to watch him die. And she cried bitterly.

We've got our own water supply. Without water anyone would die out here.

There they are! Just like the Bible said!

They look half dead. They need water fast!

Genesis 21:17-21

[17] When God heard the boy crying, the angel of God called out to Hagar from heaven and said, "Hagar, why are you worried? Don't be afraid. I have heard your son crying. [18] Help him up and hold his hand, because I will make him the father of a great nation." [19] Then God let her see a well. So she went to the well and filled the skin with water, then gave some to her son.

[20] God blessed Ishmael ...

God cared for Hagar and Ishmael as well as Isaac and his parents. God did two things for Hagar. Can you ✔ the correct answers.

❏ God helped her find a well.
❏ God took Ishmael to hospital.
❏ God sent someone to help.
❏ God gave her an important promise.
❏ God made her rich.

Captain Kate and the Hotshots sat around the computer.

God can do anything.

Abraham was mean but God helped Hagar and her son.

She was typing in all the things learned about God and Abraham and the rest of his family.

Things we have learned...

When God says something it happens!

These are real people. They lived here on earth.

God can help you anywhere. Even in the desert.

Prayer:
Is there someone you know who needs God's special help today. Pray for them now.

Something to do

What have you learned about God? Record your answer any way you like.

A sad day

I remember when my Grandmother died. Everyone was very sad, but it was a good time, too.

Something sad happened in Bible-land.

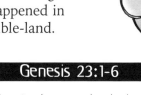

Genesis 23:1-6

When Sarah was one hundred twenty-seven years old, she died in Kiriath-Arba, better known as Hebron, in the land of Canaan. After Abraham had mourned for her, ³ he went to the Hittites and said, ⁴ "I live as a foreigner in your land, and I don't own any property where I can bury my wife. Please let me buy a piece of land."

⁵ "Sir," they answered, "you are an important man. Choose the best place to bury your wife. None of us would refuse you a resting place for your dead."

Fill in the spaces. The answers are in the Bible reading.

Sarah was _____ years old when she died.

Abraham felt very _____.

He needed to buy some _____ so he could bury Sarah.

The people thought Abraham was an _____ person.

We remembered all the special things about her. Then we said thankyou to God for all the good things in her life.

◆ Prayer:
Thank you God for giving us life. Help us to live our lives for you.

You must have been proud of her.

An important decision

The Hotshots are still in Abraham's time but Isaac has grown up and Abraham is now even older. He has an important decision to make.

It is time for his son Isaac to find a wife.

Genesis 24:1-9

Abraham was now a very old man. The Lord had made him rich, and he was successful in everything he did. ² One day, Abraham called in his most trusted servant and said to him, "Solemnly promise me ³ in the name of the Lord, who rules heaven and earth, that you won't choose a wife for my son Isaac from the people here in the land of Canaan. ⁴ Instead, go back to the land where I was born and find a wife for him from among my relatives."

⁵ But the servant asked, "What if the young woman I choose refuses to leave home and come here with me? Should I send Isaac there to look for a wife?"

⁶ "No!" Abraham answered. "Don't ever do that, no matter what. ⁷ The Lord who rules heaven brought me here from the land where I was born and promised that he would give this land to my descendants forever. When you go back there, the Lord will send his angel ahead of you to help you find a wife for my son. ⁸ If the woman refuses to come along, you don't have to keep this promise. But don't ever take my son back there." ⁹ So the servant gave Abraham his word that he would do everything he had been told to do.

Why doesn't Isaac find his own wife?

The girls here don't love and obey God. Abraham wants him to marry someone who does.

Then why won't he let Isaac go away to find a wife?

This is the land God has promised them. If Isaac left he might never come back.

Continued over page

An important decision continued ...

What an important job the servant had! Abraham knew that God would help the servant choose a good wife.

Think of a job you do.

Draw a picture of yourself doing this job.

Here's a verse about jobs. Colossians 3:23

Find it in a Bible. You could copy the words and make a mini poster.

> 23 **Do your work willingly, as though you were serving the Lord himself ...**
>
> Colossians 3:23

Prayer:
Dear God, help us always to do our best.
Help us to do our work for You.

Mei's
Research Page

Weddings

Here is some information I found about getting married. These are some of the ways people choose a partner.

Two people who love each other decide themselves to get married.

Which one of these happens where you live? Draw a circle around the heart.

A matchmaker looks for someone suitable.

Parents choose a wife or a husband for their children.

In Old Testament times a wedding started when the bridegroom travelled with his friends to the bride's house. The bride and groom were dressed in beautiful clothes. The bride wore jewels of gold and silver.

When the bride and groom returned to the groom's house, there was a huge party. Sometimes this celebration went for days.

A clever plan!

16

Genesis 24:10-14

¹⁰ Soon after that, the servant loaded ten of Abraham's camels with valuable gifts. Then he set out for the city in northern Syria, where Abraham's brother Nahor lived.

¹¹ When he got there, he let the camels rest near the well outside the city. It was late afternoon, the time when the women came out for water.
¹² The servant prayed:

You, Lord, are the God my master Abraham worships. Please keep your promise to him and let me find a wife for Isaac today. ¹³ The young women of the city will soon come to this well for water, ¹⁴ and I'll ask one of them for a drink. If she gives me a drink and then offers to get some water for my camels, I'll know she is the one you have chosen and that you have kept your promise to my master.

How did the servant show that he was trusting God?

_____

_____

_____

_____

Do you think anyone will get water for his camels?

YES / NO

We're going to follow Abraham's servant and see what he does to find a bride for Isaac.

things to kn

Camels can go for a time without food drink. They store f as fat in their hump when they need i When they come t water hole in the de they drink a great A thirsty camel c drink 114 litres o water.

Do you get worried if you think something is too hard for you? Like the servant, we should ask God for help then keep looking for the answer.

Prayer idea:
Is there something you need to do that you think is too hard? Ask God now to help you.

Mei's
Research Page

Water in Bible times

Parts of the Bible lands didn't get much rain. People had to dig down deep into the earth to find water. The well was lined with stones and had a flat rock covering it to keep the water clean. Water was precious.

Women had to walk to the well every day. There were no taps in the houses, so they had to carry all the water they needed back home in water jars. The women carried the jars on their heads or shoulders. They were heavy! The best part about collecting water was meeting friends and chatting.

You can still see some ancient wells if you go to Bible lands today. (You don't need a Time-ship!)

Is she the one?

17

📖 Genesis 24:15-21

15 While he was still praying, a beautiful unmarried young woman came by with a water jar on her shoulder. She was Rebekah, the daughter of Bethuel, the son of Abraham's brother Nahor and his wife Milcah. Rebekah walked past Abraham's servant, then went over to the well, and filled her water jar. When she started back, 17 Abraham's servant ran to her and said, "Please let me have a drink of water."

18 "I'll be glad to," she answered. Then she quickly took the jar from her shoulder and held it while he drank. 19 After he had finished, she said, "Now I'll give your camels all the water they want." She quickly poured out water for them, and she kept going back for more, until his camels had drunk all they wanted. 21 Abraham's servant did not say a word, but he watched everything Rebekah did, because he wanted to know for certain if this was the woman the Lord had chosen.

Hey! Here comes a young woman. Let's see what happens.

Which words describe Rebekah?
Circle them.

Polite Beautiful Unkind
Rude Lazy Kind Unhelpful
Married Hardworking Helpful

Prayer Idea:
Praise God for helping everyone who trusts him. Has God helped you do something hard? Say thank you or ask for help again.

Did you see that? She gave the servant something to drink, and then she went back and got water for all those camels.

She's great! What's he waiting for?

An answer to prayer

So that's why he was waiting. He knew she was beautiful and kind, and now he knows that she is from Abraham's family. She loves God. Amazing!

Genesis 24:22-27

22 The servant had brought along an expensive gold ring and two large gold bracelets. When Rebekah had finished bringing the water, he gave her the ring for her nose and the bracelets for her arms. 23 Then he said, "Please tell me who your father is. Does he have room in his house for me and my men to spend the night?"

24 She answered, "My father is Bethuel, the son of Nahor and Milcah. 25 We have a place where you and your men can stay, and we also have enough straw and feed for your camels."

26 Then the servant bowed his head and prayed, 27 "I thank you, Lord God of my master Abraham! You have led me to his relatives and kept your promise to him."

Not only that, but he now has a safe place to stay.

What have we learnt about the servant?

Did he forget about God?   YES / NO

Did he expect God to help him?   YES / NO

Did he wait until later to thank God? YES / NO

God knew the best wife for Isaac. God knows what is best for us, too. We might not be able to understand what is happening in our lives, but we do know this:

Prayer:
Dear God, you know all about us and you still love us. Thank you for your love.

God loves us and keeps his promises

19

Getting on with the job

Genesis 24:28-33

28 Rebekah ran straight home and told her family everything. 29 Her brother Laban heard her tell what the servant had said, and he saw the ring and the bracelets she was wearing. So Laban ran out to Abraham's servant, who was standing by his camels at the well. 31 Then Laban said, "The Lord has brought you safely here. Come home with me. There's no need for you to keep on standing outside. I have a room ready for you in our house, and there's also a place for your camels."

32 Abraham's servant went home with Laban, where Laban's servants unloaded his camels and gave them straw and feed. Then they brought water into the house, so Abraham's servant and his men could wash their feet. 33 After that, they brought in food. But the servant said, "Before I eat, I must tell you why I have come."

"Go ahead and tell us," Laban answered.

This is better than a movie

But it really happened.

These people really lived 4000 years ago in this part of the world.

Isn't it amazing how it's all working out?

It's just like a jigsaw puzzle with all the bits making a big picture.

God sent Rebekah along at the right time. She's just the right kind of wife for Isaac. Her family are excited about it too...

Prayer:
Dear God, thank you that you keep your promises and that you love us so much.

40

20

The servant's story – the Big Picture

Genesis 24:34-49

34 The servant explained:

I am Abraham's servant. 35 The Lord has been good to my master and has made him very rich. He has given him many sheep, goats, cattle, camels, and donkeys, as well as a lot of silver and gold, and many slaves. 36 Sarah, my master's wife, didn't have any children until she was very old. Then she had a son, and my master has given him everything. 37 I solemnly promised my master that I would do what he said. And he told me, "Don't choose a wife for my son from the women in this land of Canaan. 38 Instead, go back to the land where I was born and find a wife for my son from among my relatives."

39 I asked my master, "What if the young woman refuses to come with me?"

40 My master answered, "I have always obeyed the Lord, and he will send his angel to help you find my son a wife from among my own relatives. 41 But if they refuse to let her come back with you, then you are freed from your promise."

42 When I came to the well today, I silently prayed, "You, Lord, are the God my master Abraham worships, so please lead me to a wife for his son 43 while I am here at the well. When a young woman comes out to get water, I'll ask her to give me a drink. 44 If she gives me a drink and offers to get some water for my camels, I'll know she is the one you have chosen."

45 Even before I had finished praying, Rebekah came by with a water jar on her shoulder. When she had filled the jar, I asked her for a drink. 46 She quickly lowered the jar from her shoulder and said, "Have a drink. Then I'll get water for your camels." So I drank, and after that she got some water for my camels. 47 I asked her who her father was, and she answered, "My father is Bethuel the son of Nahor and Milcah." Right away I put the ring in her nose and the bracelets on her arms. 48 Then I bowed my head and gave thanks to the God my master Abraham worships. The Lord had led me straight to my master's relatives, and I had found a wife for his son.

49 Now please tell me if you are willing to do the right thing for my master. Will you treat him fairly, or do I have to look for another young woman?

Continued over page

The servant's story – the Big Picture
continued ...

Here is the story the servant told, but it's all mixed up.
Can you sort it out by putting the numbers 1-7 in the jigsaw
bits next to the sentences in order. Take your time and use
pencil. It's tricky!

The servant prayed
that God would show
him the right woman.

Sarah, Abraham's
wife, had a son when
she was very old.

He said,
'Choose a wife
for my son
from among my
relatives'.

Abraham
asked his
servant to
find his son
a wife.

She was the one
who offered to
get water for
the camels.

Then the
servant
thanked God
for leading him
to Abraham's
relatives.

God was good to
Abraham and made
him very rich.

*Draw the
part of the
story you
like best.*

Prayer:
Thank you God that
you know the big picture.
You care about what
happens in our lives.
Please work things out
so that I serve you best.

42

TIME TRAVEL ALERT!

21

A big decision

CREW ALERT! Alana is on the Time-ship and sees the fuel supply light flashing. What should she do? The story isn't over yet, but the fuel supply is so low it could be dangerous to stay. The others are still at Rebekah's family home.

Quick! All Aboard! There's no time to waste!

But what about Isaac and Rebekah? What happens to them?

The Bible reading tells what happened next.

Genesis 24:50-58

50 Laban and Bethuel answered, "The Lord has done this. We have no choice in the matter. 51 Take Rebekah with you; she can marry your master's son, just as the Lord has said." 52 Abraham's servant bowed down and thanked the Lord. 53 Then he gave clothing, as well as silver and gold jewellery, to Rebekah. He also gave expensive gifts to her brother and her mother.

54 Abraham's servant and the men with him ate and drank, then spent the night there. The next morning they got up, and the servant told Rebekah's mother and brother, "I would like to go back to my master now."

55 "Let Rebekah stay with us for a week or ten days," they answered. "Then she may go."

56 But he said, "Don't make me stay any longer. The Lord has already helped me find a wife for my master's son. Now let us return."

57 They answered, "Let's ask Rebekah what she wants to do." 58 They called her and asked, "Are you willing to leave with this man right now?"

"Yes," she answered.

✔ the correct answers to Mei's question:

☐ Rebekah was too shy to go with the servant.

☐ Rebekah's family wanted her to stay longer.

☐ Rebekah was ready to go right away.

Prayer: Dear God, Please help us to obey you like Rebekah did.

43

A happy ending

...Time to go. Is everyone strapped in? 21st century here we come!

> I wish we could have seen Isaac and Rebecca meet.

Genesis 24:59-67

59 So they agreed to let Rebekah and an old family servant woman leave immediately with Abraham's servant and his men. 60 They gave Rebekah their blessing and said, "We pray that God will give you many children and grandchildren and that he will help them defeat their enemies." 61 Afterwards, Rebekah and the young women who were to travel with her prepared to leave. Then they got on camels and left with Abraham's servant and his men.

63 One evening Isaac was walking out in the fields, when suddenly he saw a group of people approaching on camels. So he started toward them. Rebekah saw him coming; she got down from her camel, and asked, "Who is that man?"

"He is my master Isaac, " the servant answered. Then Rebekah covered her face with her veil.

66 The servant told Isaac everything that had happened.

Circle the people who had a part in God's plan for Abraham and his family.

> At least we have the Bible to tell us the end of the story.

Abraham's servant   Rebekah's family   the family servant

the soldier

a king   Abraham   Rebekah

They did what God wanted, even in small everyday things. God cares about the small things we do each day. Working for God doesn't just mean going to church or telling others about him. It also means obeying God in the way we live every day of our life.

Prayer Idea:
Ask God to help you listen to and obey him every day.

A one-way ticket

It's great to be home. I don't think I want to go anywhere for a long time.

You and Jonah both! He didn't want to go where God told him.

Back in the clubhouse Reuben asked about Jonah. They found the book about him in the Bible.

Tick this box when you find Jonah in your Bible.

Jonah 1:1-3

One day the Lord told Jonah, the son of Amittai, [2] to go to the great city of Nineveh and say to the people, "The Lord has seen your terrible sins. You are doomed!"

[3] Instead, Jonah ran from the Lord. He went to the seaport of Joppa and bought a ticket on a ship that was going to Spain. Then he got on the ship and sailed away to escape.

In those days Spain was a long way away. Jonah must have been really worried about the job God gave him to make him run away to Spain.

'I know how he feels,' said Suzy. 'I hate tidying my room. When Mum tells me to tidy it I always try to hide so she can't find me.'

'What happens then?' asked Alana.

'Well there's always trouble and we both get unhappy.' Suzy told her.

Prayer:
Dear God, help us to change the way we think about things. Help us to be willing to do the things we know we should do.

24 Sleeping through a Storm

The Hotshots have been on a hike.

I could go straight to sleep!

And I'm so tired I could sleep through a storm!

Funny you should say that, Reuben. That's exactly what Jonah did.

Jonah 1:4-7

4 But the Lord made a strong wind blow, and such a bad storm came up that the ship was about to be broken to pieces. 5 The sailors were frightened, and they all started praying to their gods. They even threw the ship's cargo overboard to make the ship lighter.

All this time, Jonah was down below deck, sound asleep. 6 The ship's captain went to him and said, "How can you sleep at a time like this? Get up and pray to your God! Maybe he will have pity on us and keep us from drowning."

7 Finally, the sailors got together and said, "Let's ask our gods to show us who caused all this trouble." It turned out to be Jonah.

Circle the things that happen to you when you are afraid:

laugh

knees tremble

go to sleep

Sleeping through a Storm continued ...

Someone has mixed up this story.
Write 1-5 in the boxes to show
the order it should be in.

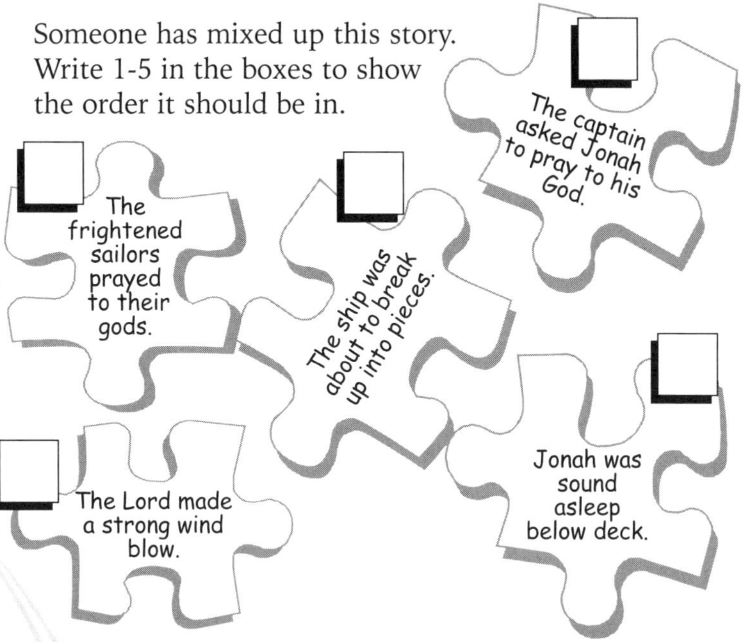

The captain asked Jonah to pray to his God.

The frightened sailors prayed to their gods.

The ship was about to break up into pieces.

The Lord made a strong wind blow.

Jonah was sound asleep below deck.

stomach hurts

face turns white

hands get sweaty

feel sick

air stands on end

teeth chatter

any others?

_____

_____

Prayer Idea:
Dear God, thank you for being with us when we are afraid.
We know that you can see us and care about us.

Running scared

The Hotshots want to hear more about Jonah.

Jonah 1:8-12

8 They started asking him, "Are you the one who brought all this trouble on us? What business are you in? Where do you come from? What is your country? Who are your people?"

9 Jonah answered, "I'm a Hebrew, and I worship the Lord God of heaven, who made the sea and the dry land."

10 When the sailors heard this, they were frightened, because Jonah had already told them he was running from the Lord. Then they said, "Do you know what you have done?"

11 The storm kept getting worse, until finally the sailors asked him, "What should we do with you to make the sea calm down?"

12 Jonah told them, "Throw me into the sea, and it will calm down. I'm the cause of this terrible storm."

Clues:

The sailors asked, 'Are you the one who brought this _ _ _ _ _ _ _ (1) on us?'
Jonah answered, 'I'm a _ _ _ _ _ _ (2).
I _ _ _ _ _ _ _ (3) the Lord _ _ _ ' (4).
Jonah was running from the _ _ _ _ (5).
The _ _ _ _ _ (6) kept getting _ _ _ _ _ (7). Jonah told the sailors to throw him _ _ _ _ (8) the sea.

Prayer:
Thank you God that You love us even when we do wrong.

Man overboard

The sailors really didn't want to throw Jonah overboard.

No. They even tried to row ashore in the storm.

And *Hotshots*! Who did the sailors pray to?

Jonah 1:13-16

[13] The sailors tried their best to row to the shore. But they could not do it, and the storm kept getting worse every minute. [14] So they prayed to the Lord, "Please don't let us drown for taking this man's life. Don't hold us guilty for killing an innocent man. All of this happened because you wanted it to." [15] Then they threw Jonah overboard, and the sea calmed down. [16] The sailors were so terrified that they offered a sacrifice to the Lord and made all kinds of promises.

They prayed:

The sailors even made promises to God. They could see God was powerful.

Prayer Idea:

Isn't it amazing that God who is so powerful is so loving? Spend some time being thankful. Tell God the way you feel.

Three days in the dark

What would you do if a giant fish swallowed you? Here's what Jonah did.

Jonah 1:17; 2:1-2

17 The Lord sent a big fish to swallow Jonah, and Jonah was inside the fish for three days and three nights.

From inside the fish, Jonah prayed to the Lord his God:

2 When I was in trouble, Lord,
1 I prayed to you,
and you listened to me.
From deep in the world
of the dead,
I begged for your help,
and you answered my prayer.

Now it's Jonah's turn to pray.

His disobedience didn't stop him. He still prayed to God.

I reckon he must be the only person who ever prayed inside a fish.

Who else was buried for three days and three nights?

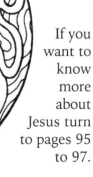

Hey! I know who. Wasn't Jesus buried for three days and nights?

Help Jonah find his way out!

If you want to know more about Jesus turn to pages 95 to 97.

(From Let's Go Puzzle Zone © Scripture Union, 1997 used with permission.)

Prayer:
Dear God, Thank you that you always listen to me when I talk to you.

28 Rescued

I remember once when I was only a little boy and I fell into a swimming pool.

My big brother dived into the pool and pulled me to the top and then dragged me out of the pool.

Jonah 2:3-9

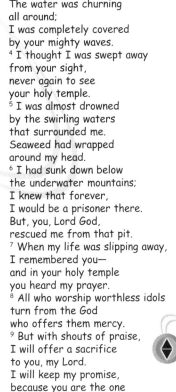

3 You threw me down
to the bottom of the sea.
The water was churning
all around;
I was completely covered
by your mighty waves.
4 I thought I was swept away
from your sight,
never again to see
your holy temple.
5 I was almost drowned
by the swirling waters
that surrounded me.
Seaweed had wrapped
around my head.
6 I had sunk down below
the underwater mountains;
I knew that forever,
I would be a prisoner there.
But, you, Lord God,
rescued me from that pit.
7 When my life was slipping away,
I remembered you—
and in your holy temple
you heard my prayer.
8 All who worship worthless idols
turn from the God
who offers them mercy.
9 But with shouts of praise,
I will offer a sacrifice
to you, my Lord.
I will keep my promise,
because you are the one
with power to save.

Jonah must have thought that he was going to drown deep down in the sea. He had disobeyed God but then God saved him.

In verse 8, Jonah used a word to describe God. It means love that we don't deserve. Fill in the blanks to make the word.

M _ R C _

Prayer Idea:
Thank you God that you show us mercy. Help us to show mercy to our family and friends.

29 A Second Chance

I found out why Jonah didn't want to go to Nineveh, where God had told him to go!

Jonah eventually went to Nineveh. Here's what happened.

Jonah 2:10; 3:1-5

¹⁰ The Lord commanded the fish to vomit up Jonah on the shore. And it did.

Jonah was really upset and angry. ² So he prayed:

Our Lord, I knew from the very beginning that you wouldn't destroy Nineveh. That's why I left my own country and headed for Spain. You are a kind and merciful God, and you are very patient. You always show love, and you don't like to punish anyone, not even foreigners.

³ Now let me die! I'd be better off dead.

⁴ The Lord replied, "What right do you have to be angry?"

⁵ Jonah then left through the east gate of the city and made a shelter to protect himself from the sun. He sat under the shelter, waiting to see what would happen to Nineveh.

Read about **Nineveh** and **wearing sackcloth** on Mei's page (opposite). How do you show you are sorry? Circle the things you do:

say sorry

cry

try to change

do something to help

talk to God about it

wear sackcloth

◆ Prayer:
Dear God. Sorry for all the things I do to hurt you. Please change me and make me more like Jesus.

Mei's Research Page

Nineveh

Nineveh was a large city in a country, which was enemies with Jonah's country. Jonah suspected that if the people said they were sorry God would forgive them. I think he wanted God to punish them. He didn't realise how much God loved them.

Wearing sackcloth

Sackcloth is cloth made from goat or camel hair and was used for grain sacks. It would have been very prickly and awful to wear.

In Bible times people sometimes took off their clothes and wore sackcloth to show how sorry they were for something they'd done. Often they would go without eating at the same time. If they weren't sorry before that they would be afterwards!

53

A big story

How many of those who lived in Nineveh do you think were sorry? You might be surprised …

Jonah 3:6-10

⁶ When the king of Nineveh heard what was happening, he also dressed in sackcloth; he left the royal palace and sat in dust. ⁷ Then he and his officials sent out an order for everyone in the city to obey. It said:

None of you or your animals may eat or drink a thing. Each of you must wear sackcloth, and you must even put sackcloth on your animals.

You must also pray to the Lord God with all your heart and stop being sinful and cruel. Maybe God will change his mind and have mercy on us, so we won't be destroyed.

¹⁰ When God saw that the people had stopped doing evil things, he had pity and did not destroy them as he had planned.

Have a go at drawing the scene in Nineveh yourself.

What a sight that must have bee Hey Hotshots! Hov about we do a huge drawing of what th King and his people would have looked lik Don't forget the animals too.

There's an interesting verse in the reading today.
Find it and finish the words:

When _ _ _ saw that the _ _ _ _ _ _
had stopped doing _ _ _ _ things, He had
_ _ _ _ and did not _ _ _ _ _ _ _ _ them
as He had planned.

Prayer:
Dear God,
Thank you
that you
show pity
and mercy.
Help me to
treat others
like that.

God is love

Jonah is just the opposite of God. God shows the foreigners in Nineveh kindness and mercy and love.

Jonah is so angry that he wants to die!

I'm not always kind to people who come from another country. Sometimes kids at school laugh and make fun of people who are different.

Jonah 4:1-5

Jonah was really upset and angry. ² So he prayed:

Our Lord, I knew from the very beginning that you wouldn't destroy Nineveh. That's why I left my own country and headed for Spain. You are a kind and merciful God, and you are very patient. You always show love, and you don't like to punish anyone, not even foreigners.

³ Now let me die! I'd be better off dead.

⁴ The Lord replied, "What right do you have to be angry?"

⁵ Jonah then left through the east gate of the city and made a shelter to protect himself from the sun. He sat under the shelter, waiting to see what would happen to Nineveh.

Here is a great verse to try to remember. It is in Jonah chapter 4, verse 2.

Cross out all the X's.

YouxarexaxkindxandxmercifulxGod,xand
xYouxarexveryxpatient.xYouxalwaysxshow
xlove,xandxyouxdon'txlikextoxpunish
xanyone,xnotxevenxforeigners.

Prayer:
Dear God, help me to show love and kindness to people who are different.

A lesson to learn

⁶ The Lord made a vine grow up to shade Jonah's head and protect him from the sun. Jonah was very happy to have the vine, ⁷ but early the next morning the Lord sent a worm to chew on the vine, and the vine dried up. ⁸ During the day the Lord sent a scorching wind, and the sun beat down on Jonah's head, making him feel faint. Jonah was ready to die, and he shouted, "I wish I were dead!"

⁹ But the Lord asked, "Jonah, do you have the right to be angry about the vine?"

"Yes, I do," he answered, "and I'm angry enough to die."

¹⁰ But the Lord said:
You are concerned about a vine that you did not plant or take care of, a vine that grew up in one night and died the next.

Make a list of things that are important to you:

_____

_____

_____

Are these things more important than people?
YES / NO

What was more important to Jonah?
The vine / the people

What was more important to God?
The vine / the people

Think of someone you know who needs someone to be their friend. Write down one thing you could do to show that you care about them.

Jonah was angry with God because He showed mercy. Do friends ever get angry at you for not doing what they want?
YES / NO

◆ Prayer Idea:
Sometimes it's hard to know what to do, especially when we're sad or angry. Here's a prayer you could pray:
Please God, help me to do what's right, even when I don't feel like it. Help me to please you always. Amen.

Another adventure

Captain Kate has called a meeting of the *Hotshots*. It's time for another adventure in the Time Machine. Prepare to meet another person in Bible History.

Colour the shapes with a dot to discover his name.

The Hotshots are going to the land where Jesus lived. The time? Just after Jesus went back to heaven. That's over 1950 years ago.

Sean has been drawing up maps of Palestine.

Reuben has collected clothes to help the time travellers blend in with the crowds. Alana has completed refuelling, and Suzy is ready to bring the *Hotshot* into action.

Checklist

All aboard! It's through time we travel! ......

Mei's
Research Page

Peter

Mei has found out all she could about Peter.

Peter was a fisherman when Jesus met him. Jesus called him and he left his job and joined Jesus. He was one of the special group of three with James and John.

Sometimes Peter was brave and strong. Other times he was scared and a coward. Once he said he didn't know Jesus.

After Jesus went back to heaven and sent the Holy Spirit, Peter changed. He was full of courage.

He became a missionary. Peter travelled around to different places and was an important preacher. Peter also told the Jewish authorities about Jesus. He would have to be very brave to do this.

The name Peter means 'rock'.

Map

Sean has included a map for you to follow Peter's travels. The first place the *Hotshots* plan to visit is Lydda.

Italy
• Rome

Macedonia

Thessalonica Philippi

Galatia

Corinth Athens Colossae Tarsus • Haran
• Antioch

Sicily

Malta

Crete Cyprus

Mediterranean Sea • Damascus Ur
Caesarea Sea of Galilee
Joppa Canaan
Jerusalem Dead Sea

Libya Lydda

Egypt

Red Sea

Who heals?

33

The *Hotshots* have travelled back through time and changed into their new outfits. They are in Lydda. Can you locate Lydda on the map on page 59.

Here's what happened just before the Hotshots arrived.

Acts 9:32-35

32 While Peter was travelling from place to place, he visited the Lord's followers who lived in the town of Lydda. 33 There he met a man named Aeneas, who for eight years had been sick in bed and could not move. 34 Peter said to Aeneas, "Jesus Christ has healed you! Get up and make up your bed." Right away he stood up.

35 Many people in the towns of Lydda and Sharon saw Aeneas and became followers of the Lord.

Now the Hotshots are listening to people tell the story of what Peter did. Everyone is very excited. They think Peter made the paralysed man walk.

Who did Peter say healed the man?

If you want to know more about Jesus go to page 95 (About Jesus).

Prayer:
Thankyou God that you have the power to heal.

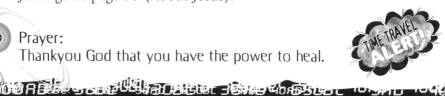

TIME TRAVEL ALERT!

Cornelius from Caesarea

Mei told the Hotshots about the Roman army.

Acts 10:1-8

In Caesarea there was a man named Cornelius, who was the captain of a group of soldiers called "The Italian Unit."
[2] Cornelius was a very religious man. He worshiped God, and so did everyone else who lived in his house. He had given a lot of money to the poor and was always praying to God.

[3] One afternoon at about three o'clock, Cornelius had a vision. He saw an angel from God coming to him and calling him by name.
[4] Cornelius was surprised and stared at the angel. Then he asked, "What is this all about?"

The angel answered, "God has heard your prayers and knows about your gifts to the poor. [5] Now send some men to Joppa for a man named Simon Peter. [6] He is visiting with Simon the leather maker, who lives in a house near the sea." [7] After saying this, the angel left.

Cornelius called in two of his servants and one of his soldiers who worshiped God. [8] He explained everything to them and sent them off to Joppa.

Underline the place where Cornelius was.

The Bible lands at this time were under the control of Rome. Roman soldiers walked the streets.

A Roman centurion was an important soldier from Rome who was in charge of 100 men.

Cornlius was called a Gentile. That means he was not one of the Jewish people. But Cornelius was a religious man. He gave money to the poor and he prayed to God.

Find the city he came from on the map on page 59. Now find Joppa on your map. That's where Cornelius sent two servants and a soldier to find Peter.

Prayer Idea:
Do you know any Christians from other countries? You might like to pray for them now. You could pray that they will listen to what God is saying to them.

TIME TRAVEL ALERT!

God communicates

When Kate and the Hotshots read the Bible they often feel God is telling them something. In the Bible God often told people things through dreams and visions.

God spoke to Cornelius that way. Remember? What did he tell him?

Now read how God spoke to Peter in a vision too.

Acts 10:9-16

9 The next day about noon these men were coming near Joppa. Peter went up on the roof of the house to pray 10 and became very hungry. While the food was being prepared, he fell sound asleep and had a vision. 11 He saw heaven open, and something came down like a huge sheet held up by its four corners. 12 In it were all kinds of animals, snakes, and birds. 13 A voice said to him, "Peter, get up! Kill these and eat them."

14 But Peter said, "Lord, I can't do that! I've never eaten anything that is unclean and not fit to eat15 The voice spoke to him again, "When God says that something can be used for food, don't say it isn't fit to eat."

16 This happened three times before the sheet was suddenly taken back to heaven.

Prayer:
Dear God, please help me to know when You are speaking to me and to understand what you are saying. Help me to listen for you when I read the Bible and all through the day.

What do you think God was trying to tell Peter?

The Jews were taught not to eat certain foods because they were 'unclean'. The animals in Peter's dream were the 'unclean' animals they were not allowed to eat.

The Jews believed people who came from different countries were 'unclean'. They thought they should stay away from them.

What do you think the dream meant? Cross out the wrong ones.

God was telling Peter not to eat meat from these animals.

God was saying Peter should keep away from Gentiles.

God was saying it was now OK to eat meat from these animals.

God was saying Peter should spend time with Gentiles (not Jews).

63

36

Just as God said

The Hotshots watched the visitors at Peter's house. They were not even Jews, but Peter invited them to stay overnight at his house. The next day Peter left with them for Joppa.

Acts 10:17-23

[17] Peter was still wondering what all of this meant, when the men sent by Cornelius came and stood at the gate. They had found their way to Simon's house [18] and were asking if Simon Peter was staying there.

[19] While Peter was still thinking about the vision, the Holy Spirit said to him, "Three men are here looking for you. [20] Hurry down and go with them. Don't worry, I sent them."

[21] Peter went down and said to the men, "I am the one you are looking for. Why have you come?"

[22] They answered, "Captain Cornelius sent us. He is a good man who worships God and is liked by the Jewish people. One of God's holy angels told Cornelius to send for you, so he could hear what you have to say." [23] Peter invited them to spend the night.

The next morning, Peter and some of the Lord's followers in Joppa left with the men who had come from Cornelius.

Mei remembers the first time she went to her new school. She only spoke a little bit of English, and was feeling very strange in her new country. Not many of the other children talked to her. But she soon became friends with Alana and Suzy, who were always friendly and smiled at her.

Think of all the people in your school. Write down the countries they have come from:

Prayer: Please God help me to be especially friendly to people who have come from another country

_____

_____

Peter and Cornelius

The Hotshots travelled to Caesarea and found Cornelius' house. Cornelius had invited lots of friends and relations to hear what Peter had to say. The Hotshots went in without being noticed. The Bible reading will tell you what they saw and heard.

Acts 10:25-33

²⁵When Peter arrived, Cornelius greeted him. Then he knelt at Peter's feet and started worshiping him. ²⁶ But Peter took hold of him and said, "Stand up! I am nothing more than a human."

²⁷ As Peter entered the house, he was still talking with Cornelius. Many people were there, ²⁸ and Peter said to them, "You know that we Jews are not allowed to have anything to do with other people. But God has shown me that he doesn't think anyone is unclean or unfit. ²⁹ I agreed to come here, but I want to know why you sent for me."

³⁰ Cornelius answered:

Four days ago at about three o'clock in the afternoon I was praying at home. Suddenly a man in bright clothes stood in front of me. ³ He said, "Cornelius, God has heard your prayers, and he knows about your gifts to the poor. ³² Now send to Joppa for Simon Peter. He is visiting in the home of Simon the leather maker, who lives near the sea."

³³ I sent for you right away, and you have been good enough to come. All of us are here in the presence of the Lord God, so that we can hear what he has to say.

See if you can work out what Peter said.

anyone think is doesn't unclean God or unfit

Prayer idea: God wants to communicate with us but we don't always listen. You might like to just be still for a while and think what God might be saying to you.

38 Good News

Acts 10:34-43

34 Peter then said:

Now I am certain that God treats all people alike. 35 God is pleased with everyone who worships him and does right, no matter what nation they come from. 36 This is the same message that God gave to the people of Israel, when he sent Jesus Christ, the Lord of all, to offer peace to them.

37 You surely know what happened everywhere in Judea. It all began in Galilee after John had told everyone to be baptised. 38 God gave the Holy Spirit and power to Jesus from Nazareth. He was with Jesus, as he went around doing good and healing everyone who was under the power of the devil. 39 We all saw what Jesus did both in Israel and in the city of Jerusalem.

Jesus was put to death on a cross. 40 But three days later, God raised him to life and let him be seen. 41 Not everyone saw him. He was seen only by us, who ate and drank with him after he was raised from death. We were the ones God chose to tell others about him.

42 God told us to announce clearly to the people that Jesus is the one he has chosen to judge the living and the dead. 43 Every one of the prophets has said that all who have faith in Jesus will have their sins forgiven in his name.

Everything is starting to make sense. Peter has learned that God treats all people alike, no matter where they come from.

Cornelius has learned about the special plan that God has for the world. He heard that Jesus died and came back to life so we can be right with God. Jesus has made a way for us to be forgiven and have a fresh start as one of God's family.

Work out what Peter and Cornelius have discovered about God:

EVE RYPER SONIN THE WORL DIS LOV ED BYG ODAND CANJ OING OD'SFAM ILY

_____

_____ ,

_____

A Special Event

Acts 10:44-48

⁴⁴ While Peter was still speaking, the Holy Spirit took control of everyone who was listening. ⁴⁵ Some Jewish followers of the Lord had come with Peter, and they were surprised that the Holy Spirit had been given to Gentiles. ⁴⁶ Now they were hearing Gentiles speaking unknown languages and praising God.

Peter said, ⁴⁷ "These Gentiles have been given the Holy Spirit, just as we have! I am certain that no one would dare stop us from baptizing them." ⁴⁸ Peter ordered them to be baptised in the name of Jesus Christ, and they asked him to stay on for a few days.

The *Hotshots* are back in the time-ship returning to base. They are talking about the exciting thing that just happened. As Peter was telling about Jesus, God's Spirit came into everyone who was listening, and the Hotshots saw them all begin to praise God.

The Jews were amazed because the same thing had happened to them. God was showing them that Jews and Gentiles could become part of God's family! God has no favourites.

These exciting things wouldn't have happened if Peter and Cornelius had not obeyed God.

Put these words into the right order to make a sentence:

CORNELIUS BECAME HIS AND
CHRISTIANS FAMILY

 Prayer: Thankyou God for sending Jesus to show us how to be part of your family.

The book of Acts

The Hotshots are finding out about the book of Acts in their Bibles.

'It's all about the very first churches,' Kate told them. 'It tells the stories of how the good news about Jesus spread after Jesus went back to heaven.'

Some of the Christians ran away from Jerusalem because people were trying to kill them for talking about Jesus. They spread the message wherever they went. Some went to Antioch which was about 500 kilometres to the north. Many people became followers of Jesus in Antioch.

The Good News Spreads

19 Some of the Lord's followers had been scattered because of the terrible trouble that started when Stephen was killed. They went as far as Phoenicia, Cyprus, and Antioch, but they told the message only to the Jews.

20 Some of the followers from Cyprus and Cyrene went to Antioch and started telling Gentiles about the Lord Jesus. 21 The Lord's power was with them, and many people turned to the Lord and put their faith in him.

Mei? Who was Stephen and what happened to him?

Stephen loved Jesus. Seven men were chosen to be leaders in the early church and Stephen was one. He was full of faith and very wise.

The Jewish leaders didn't like what Stephen was saying about Jesus, so they stoned him to death. Before he died Stephen prayed that God would forgive those who killed him.

Draw what you think Stephen and Peter looked like. We can't be sure, but because of the part of the world they came from, they probably had dark hair and brown eyes.

WANTED!
by Jewish leaders

Peter | Stephen

Something to do

Read the full story of Stephen in Acts chapters 6 and 7 in your Bible.

◆ Prayer:
Dear God, help me tell my friends about Jesus.

Barnabas and Saul

The *Hotshots* have decided to start a *Hotshots* Gallery where they will hang paintings or drawings of the people in these stories. They already have pictures of Peter and Stephen. Mei is ready to tell about Barnabas and Saul.

Acts 11:22-26

22 News of what was happening reached the church in Jerusalem. Then they sent Barnabas to Antioch.

23 When Barnabas got there and saw what God had been kind enough to do for them, he was very glad. So he begged them to remain faithful to the Lord with all their hearts. 24 Barnabas was a good man of great faith, and he was filled with the Holy Spirit. Many more people turned to the Lord.

25 Barnabas went to Tarsus to look for Saul. 26 He found Saul and brought him to Antioch, where they met with the church for a whole year and taught many of its people. There in Antioch the Lord's followers were first called Christians.

Mei's Research Page

Here's what I have discovered about Barnabas and Saul.

Barnabas

was a kind person who cared for people and encouraged them. He was a missionary to the Gentiles (Gentiles were all the people who weren't Jews. Jesus was a Jew. Peter an Jonah and Abrahan were too.) Some o the people he encouraged were Saul and his cous John Mark.

Saul

was a Jew who was born in Tarsus.
He was a Roman citizen.
He used to hunt down Christians and put them in prison.
When Saul became a Christian his life changed. He was filled with God's love. He is the world's most famous missionary.

42

Peter in Prison

At that time King Herod caused terrible suffering for some members of the church. ² He ordered soldiers to cut off the head of James, the brother of John. ³ When Herod saw that this pleased the Jewish people, he had Peter arrested during the Festival of Thin Bread. ⁴ He put Peter in jail and ordered four squads of soldiers to guard him. Herod planned to put him on trial in public after the festival.

⁵ While Peter was being kept in jail, the church never stopped praying to God for him.

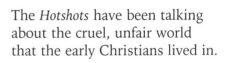

The *Hotshots* have been talking about the cruel, unfair world that the early Christians lived in.

'Sometimes people now are just as cruel,' Reuben reminded them. 'What about the groups of children at school who think it's fun to laugh at the little kids or anyone who is a bit different. They are just as cruel as Herod.'

Why did Herod do these terrible things? *Cross out the wrong ones. (Check verse 3.)*

❏ He hated these people.
❏ He thought it was a joke to hurt people.
❏ He thought the Jews would like him for hurting the Christians.
❏ He wanted to be popular.

What were the Christians doing? *Tick the right one.*

❏ They were hiding.
❏ They were crying.
❏ They were praying to God.
❏ They were fighting.

Prayer:
Dear God, please help me to be brave and pray when I am in trouble.

Rescue

Here's something that really happened whether you believe it or not!

I've drawn this story but the drawings are all mixed up. Help me to put them in the correct order.

Acts: 12:6-11

6 The night before Peter was to be put on trial, he was asleep and bound by two chains. A soldier was guarding him on each side, and two other soldiers were guarding the entrance to the jail. 7 Suddenly an angel from the Lord appeared, and light flashed around in the cell. The angel poked Peter in the side and woke him up. Then he said, "Quick! Get up!"

The chains fell off his hands, 8 and the angel said, "Get dressed and put on your sandals." Peter did what he was told. Then the angel said, "Now put on your coat and follow me." 9 Peter left with the angel, but he thought everything was only a dream. 10 They went past the two groups of soldiers, and when they came to the iron gate to the city, it opened by itself. They went out and were going along the street, when all at once the angel disappeared.

11 Peter now realized what had happened, and he said, "I am certain that the Lord sent his angel to rescue me from Herod and from everything the Jewish leaders planned to do to me."

○ Peter gets dressed and leaves.

○ An angel appears and wakes him up.

○ They walk out onto the street.

Peter realises that he is awake and that the Lord has rescued him.

○ Peter is in jail bound by two chains with soldiers guarding him.

○ The chains fall off his hands.

The gates of prison

Who was more powerful, King Herod or the Lord?

Who should we trust, other people or the Lord?

 Prayer idea:

Isn't it great to belong to God who is more powerful than anyone else? Think about God's power, then thank God for caring for you.

A visitor at night

The *Hotshots* have seen Sean's drawings. They want to know what happened next.

Acts 12:12-19

¹² Then Peter went to the house of Mary the mother of John whose other name was Mark. Many of the Lord's followers had come together there and were praying.

¹³ Peter knocked on the gate, and a servant named Rhoda came to answer. ¹⁴ When she heard Peter's voice, she was too excited to open the gate. She ran back into the house and said that Peter was standing there.

¹⁵ "You are crazy!" everyone told her. But she kept saying that it was Peter. Then they said, "It must be his angel." ¹⁶ But Peter kept on knocking, until finally they opened the gate. They saw him and were completely amazed.

¹⁷ Peter motioned for them to keep quiet. Then he told how the Lord had led him out of jail. He also said, "Tell James and the others what has happened." After that, he left and went somewhere else.

¹⁸ The next morning the soldiers who had been on guard were terribly worried and wondered what had happened to Peter. ¹⁹ Herod ordered his own soldiers to search for him, but they could not find him. Then he questioned the guards and had them put to death. After this, Herod left Judea to stay in Caesarea for a while.

You can draw the rest of the story:

1. Peter knocking on Mary's door.

2. Rhoda's face when she saw Peter.

Continued over page

A visitor at night continued ...

4. Peter still knocking on the door.

4. Peter telling his friends what happened.

5. The soldiers searching for Peter.

Peter's friends were amazed that their prayers had been answered.

God wants us to pray for other people. *Write down the names of three friends to pray for.*

_____

_____

_____

Prayer idea:
Think about these three friends. What would God want for them? (If you're not sure what to pray for, ask God to help them love others and God more. That's something God wants for everyone.)

Another missionary

We have already met Barnabas and Saul. Who is John Mark?

Acts 12:24-25

24 God's message kept spreading. 25 And after Barnabas and Saul had done the work they were sent to do, they went back to Jerusalem with John, whose other name was Mark.

Herod and his soldiers, and the Jewish leaders were doing everything they could to stop the news about Jesus spreading. Faithful people like the ones in the gallery were telling others, even though it was dangerous. The message had spread as far as Antioch and eventually it would spread all around the world.

Prayer:
Dear God, Thank you for the good news. Thank you that nothing can stop your plan for everyone to know about Jesus.

John Mark

was a Jew. His mother's name was Mary. The Christians used to meet in her house. Peter went to her house after he left the prison. Barnabas took John Mark with him on some of his journeys. John Mark also visited Paul when he was a prisoner in Rome.

Draw what you think John Mark looked like for the *Hotshots* gallery.

Mei's Research Page

75

46 Chosen for a special job

Acts 13:1-3

The church at Antioch had several prophets and teachers. They were Barnabas, Simeon, also called Niger, Lucius from Cyrene, Manaen, who was Herod's close friend, and Saul. ² While they were worshiping the Lord and going without eating, the Holy Spirit told them, "Appoint Barnabas and Saul to do the work for which I have chosen them." ³ Everyone prayed and went without eating for a while longer. Next, they placed their hands on Barnabas and Saul to show that they had been appointed to do this work. Then everyone sent them on their way.

Remember how God promised Abraham that his family would become a great nation?

God's promise became even greater. It also included non Jews, who weren't from Abraham's family.

Peter discovered this plan in the dream God gave him. The people in Antioch were ready to do what God wanted. They came from different countries, but they belonged to God's family.

Fill in the missing words:
God's plan was that ____ people would be part of His family.
The first missionaries who travelled the world were _____ and _____. Their friends prayed for them and sent them on their way.

Prayer:
Thank you God that people all over the world belong to your family. Please be with all those who are spreading your message today, especially in countries where it is dangerous.

What is really exciting is that God's plan is still coming true! Churches are still sending out missionaries today. Do you know any missionaries?

47 A sad story

The people in the Bible are not always perfect. They are real people like us. Saul was a very religious person but he did some terrible things. Find out what he was doing.

⁵⁴ When the council members heard Stephen's speech, they were angry and furious. ⁵⁵ But Stephen was filled with the Holy Spirit. He looked toward heaven, where he saw our glorious God and Jesus standing at his right side. ⁵⁶ Then Stephen said, "I see heaven open and the Son of Man standing at the right side of God!"

⁵⁷ The council members shouted and covered their ears. At once they all attacked Stephen ⁵⁸ and dragged him out of the city. Then they started throwing stones at him. The men who had brought charges against him put their coats at the feet of a young man named Saul.

Stephen was the first person to die because of his faith in Jesus. Since then, many many people have died rather than give up their faith.

These people are called martyrs.

In the Bible, Jesus says that everyone who believes in him will LIVE even if they die.

Why didn't God stop them killing Stephen?

Stephen was the first Christian martyr.

Something to do

Find John 11:25 in your Bible.
Is Suzy right?   YES   NO

Prayer idea:
Ask God to help you trust him whatever happens.

77

48 He thought he was right

Reuben walked into the garage shouting angrily ...

Sean, I'll *never* lend you anything again!

You said you were going to give my new glider plane back to me yesterday and you haven't.

I can't trust you any more. Don't think you are still my friend!

I *did* give it back. I put it in your backpack yesterday before you left school

Sean tried to say something but Reuben kept on shouting. 'You should have given it back when you said you would!'

Eventually Reuben calmed down enough to listen to what Sean was trying to tell him.

He thought he was right
continued ...

Reuben took off his backpack, looked inside it and started to turn red.

He looked up at Sean and muttered, 'Ah! Er... Sorry, Sean. You're right ... It is in here. I've got a big mouth!'

Reuben looked so sorry that everyone laughed.

Sometimes we are so sure we are right that we don't listen to what others say. It's only later that we see how wrong we are. Then we are sorry. Sometimes we even lose friends that way.

Saul was a very clever man, but he couldn't understand about Jesus. Saul became very angry with the Christians, because he thought they were wrong. Read the Bible bit to see what he did to them.

Acts 8:1-3

Saul approved the stoning of Stephen. Some faithful followers of the Lord buried Stephen and mourned very much for him.

[1] At that time the church in Jerusalem suffered terribly. All of the Lord's followers, except the apostles, were scattered everywhere in Judea and Samaria. [3] Saul started making a lot of trouble for the church. He went from house to house, arresting men and women and putting them in jail.

Prayer:
Dear God, Please help me to stay calm and to listen to what others say. Help me to understand the truth.

More trouble

Saul was so enthusiastic about his job that he even went to Damascus.

Acts 9:1-2

Saul kept on threatening to kill the Lord's followers. He even went to the high priest [2] and asked for letters to their leaders in Damascus. He did this because he wanted to arrest and take to Jerusalem any man or woman who had accepted the Lord's Way.

What was Saul planning to do in Damascus?

_____

_____

Mei's
Research Page

Damascus

was about 200 kilometres north-east of Jerusalem. It would have a week on horseback and much longer on foot.

The city was a quite a way from Jerusalem, but many Jews lived there. The city had many Jewish meeting places called synagogues.

The early Christians

were called many different things. Even the name 'Christian' was first used as a nickname. The Christians soon became proud of the name and used it themselves.

Christians were also called:

- friends of Jesus
- followers of the Way
- people of the Way
- believers

Something to do

Look up what Jesus told his friends about the Way in John 14:6

Tick this box when you have read it.

Prayer:
Dear Jesus, Thank You that You are the Way. Please help me to go your way all my life.

50

A mind blowing experience

Acts 9:3-9

³ When Saul had almost reached Damascus, a bright light from heaven suddenly flashed around him. ⁴ He fell to the ground and heard a voice that said, "Saul! Saul! Why are you so cruel to me?"

⁵ "Who are you?" Saul asked.
"I am Jesus," the Lord answered. "I am the one you are so cruel to. ⁶ Now get up and go into the city, where you will be told what to do."

⁷ The men with Saul stood there speechless. They had heard the voice, but they had not seen anyone. ⁸ Saul got up from the ground, and when he opened his eyes, he could not see a thing. Someone then led him by the hand to Damascus, ⁹ and for three days he was blind and did not eat or drink.

It looked as if nothing could stop Saul's plan. But Someone did.

If you were Paul, what do you think would have surprised you most?

How do you think you would feel after this experience?

dizzy

angry

proud

sorry

confused

frightened

ashamed

amazed

When Reuben blamed Sean for not returning his glider, Sean was hurt. His other friends were also hurt because they knew that Reuben was not being fair. Who else would have been hurt?

God understands how we feel. When we are hurting He is also hurting. He wants us to be friends with each other and to show love and care, even to people who are not our friends.

Prayer:
Dear Jesus, It's easy to love my friends. Help me to show love to people who aren't my friends too.

ALL ABOARD!
The *Hotshots* are preparing for another adventure. Would you like to join them? This time they're off to Damascus to see if they can find Saul.

A new beginning

Home of Ananias

What's going on in this house? The Bible records what happened here in the 1st century.

Acts 9:10-15

[10] A follower named Ananias lived in Damascus, and the Lord spoke to him in a vision. Ananias answered, "Lord, here I am."

[11] The Lord said to him, "Get up and go to the house of Judas on Straight Street. When you get there, you will find a man named Saul from the city of Tarsus. Saul is praying, [12] and he has seen a vision. He saw a man named Ananias coming to him and putting his hands on him, so that he could see again."

[13] Ananias replied, "Lord, a lot of people have told me about the terrible things this man has done to your followers in Jerusalem. [14] Now the chief priests have given him the power to come here and arrest anyone who worships in your name."

[15] The Lord said to Ananias, "Go! I have chosen him to tell foreigners, kings, and the people of Israel about me.

Circle how you think Ananias felt?

A new beginning continued ...

Here's the rest of the story. Find out what Ananias did.

Acts 9:17-19

[17] Ananias left and went into the house where Saul was staying. Ananias placed his hands on him and said, "Saul, the Lord Jesus has sent me. He is the same one who appeared to you along the road. He wants you to be able to see and to be filled with the Holy Spirit."

[18] Suddenly something like fish scales fell from Saul's eyes, and he could see. He got up and was baptized.
[19] Then he ate and felt much better.

Do you know now? *Tick the correct one.*

❏ Ananias sailed away on a boat.

❏ Ananias ran and told the soldiers.

❏ Ananias climbed over the wall to escape.

❏ Ananias went straight to Saul.

What two things did Saul do when he could see again?

1. _____

2. _____

Prayer:
Dear God, help me to obey You even when I am scared.

52

Paul in a basket

I've just heard some of the Jews planning to kill Saul. They are angry with him for preaching about Jesus.

The Hotshots are interested to see what Saul will do next. He's changed so much since he met Jesus. Instead of trying to stop the message about Jesus, he's spreading it!

Reuben has read about this in the Bible.

I bet Saul escapes ... in a most unusual way!

Read the rest of the story and draw what happened in the frame.

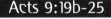

Acts 9:19b-25

For several days Saul stayed with the Lord's followers in Damascus. ²⁰ Soon he went to the Jewish meeting places and started telling people that Jesus is the Son of God. ²¹ Everyone who heard Saul was amazed and said, "Isn't this the man who caused so much trouble for those people in Jerusalem who worship in the name of Jesus? Didn't he come here to arrest them and take them to the chief priests?"

²² Saul preached with such power that he completely confused the Jewish people in Damascus, as he tried to show them that Jesus is the Messiah.

²³ Later some of them made plans to kill Saul, ²⁴ but he found out about it. He learned that they were guarding the gates of the city day and night in order to kill him. ²⁵ Then one night his followers let him down over the city wall in a large basket.

Prayer:
Thank you God for friends who can help when we are in trouble. Help me be a good friend to others.

All aboard again! We're off to Jerusalem to see what happened to Saul after he escaped.

53

Barnabas again!

Saul left and went to Caesarea, and then to Tarsus. He is getting around the country fast. Can you find those places on the map on page 59.

The time-ship has landed in the temple area in Jerusalem at the time of Saul. They are amazed at the beautiful marble buildings.

They are amazed at what they hear about Saul too. He's become a follower of Jesus!

Most people found that very hard to believe.

Saul is preaching about Jesus. The Jewish leaders won't like that. He'd better get a basket ready!

Tarsus

Cyprus

Damascus

Caesarea, Sea of Galilee

Joppa, Canaan

Acts 9:26-27

26 When Saul arrived in Jerusalem, he tried to join the followers. But they were all afraid of him, because they did not believe he was a true follower. 27 Then Barnabas helped him by taking him to the apostles. He explained how Saul had seen the Lord and how the Lord had spoken to him. Barnabas also said that when Saul was in Damascus, he had spoken bravely in the name of Jesus.

Prayer:
Dear God, Show me ways to build friendship and trust just like Barnabas did.

Hadn't Saul changed! Match the before and after jigsaw puzzle pieces.

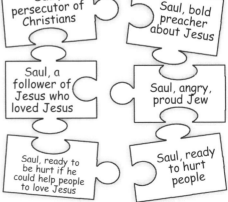

Saul, persecutor of Christians

Saul, bold preacher about Jesus

Saul, a follower of Jesus who loved Jesus

Saul, angry, proud Jew

Saul, ready to be hurt if he could help people to love Jesus

Saul, ready to hurt people

54

'Call me Paul'

The Hotshots decided to look for Saul. There were things they wanted to know about his new life. The first thing he told them was...

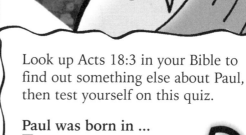

Call me Paul. I'm a changed person s I've changed my name

Read the Bible bit to find out what else he told them.

Acts 22:3

[3] I am a Jew, born and raised in the city of Tarsus in Cilicia. I was a student of Gamaliel and was taught to follow every single law of our ancestors. In fact, I was just as eager to obey God as any of you are today.

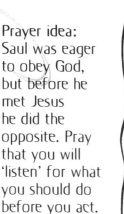

Prayer idea: Saul was eager to obey God, but before he met Jesus he did the opposite. Pray that you will 'listen' for what you should do before you act.

Look up Acts 18:3 in your Bible to find out something else about Paul, then test yourself on this quiz.

Paul was born in ...
- ❏ Jerusalem
- ❏ Rome
- ❏ Tarsus

He was a ...
- ❏ butcher
- ❏ baker
- ❏ tent maker

He was eager to ...
- ❏ obey God
- ❏ make trouble
- ❏ get rich

55 More about Paul

Paul didn't always escape trouble. He spent many years in prison for preaching about Jesus. In prison he wrote letters to churches and friends. Many of the letters he wrote are in the Bible.

Can you find Paul's letters in the contents page of your Bible? If you are not sure, ask someone to help you.
Write YES in the box when you have found them.

Some letters were written to churches in towns and cities around the Mediterranean sea. Find these places on the map on page 59.

Rome   Colossae   Galatia

Corinth   Thessalonica

The time-ship is going to one of these towns right now.

All aboard!

Ephesus

Philippi

Cars, electric lights? Did Philippi have all that in Paul's time?

Oops, wrong time. That's the year 2000.

Back in the time-ship!

Continued over page

85

More about Paul continued ...

Read what Paul wrote to the Christians in Philippi in the 1st century.

Philippians 3:5b-7

⁵ I was circumcised when I was eight days old, and I am from the nation of Israel and the tribe of Benjamin. I am a true Hebrew. As a Pharisee, I strictly obeyed the Law of Moses. ⁶ And I was so eager that I even made trouble for the church. I did everything the Law demands in order to please God.

⁷ But Christ has shown me that what I once thought was valuable is worthless.

Remember that Paul used to think he was better than anyone else.

I am Jesus...

Now he thought nothing about him was good compared with Jesus.

Fill in the missing letters to finish what he said:

B_T CHR_ST H_S SH_WN M_ THA_ WH_T I _NCE TH_ _GHT W_S V_L_ _BL_ _S W_RTHL_SS.

What was valuable to Paul after he meet Jesus?
Look up Philippians 3:8 to check your answer.

_____

Prayer:
Dear God, Help me to look for what is truly valuable in my life.

56 Paul tells all

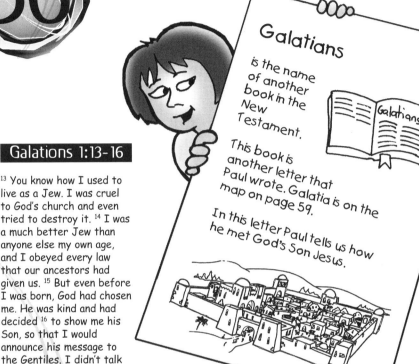

Galatians is the name of another book in the New Testament.

This book is another letter that Paul wrote. Galatia is on the map on page 59.

In this letter Paul tells us how he met God's Son Jesus.

Galations 1:13-16

13 You know how I used to live as a Jew. I was cruel to God's church and even tried to destroy it. 14 I was a much better Jew than anyone else my own age, and I obeyed every law that our ancestors had given us. 15 But even before I was born, God had chosen me. He was kind and had decided 16 to show me his Son, so that I would announce his message to the Gentiles. I didn't talk this over with anyone.

When did God choose Paul?
(verse 15)

Why did God choose Paul?
(verse 16)

If you are interested in finding out more about becoming one of God's family, turn to page 95, *Beginning with Jesus*.

Prayer:
Thank you God that you care so much about us. Help us to show Your love to other people.

57 Paul in Antioch

Just head
the synago
church

The *Hotshots* have moved on to Antioch in the time-ship. They are trying to keep up with Paul in his travels. They have noticed that when Paul arrives in a new city he always goes to the synagogue church to preach about God's plan to send Jesus.

Acts 13: 42-45

[42] As Paul and Barnabas were leaving the meeting, the people begged them to say more about these same things on the next Sabbath. [43] After the service, many Jews and a lot of Gentiles who worshiped God went with them. Paul and Barnabas begged them all to remain faithful to God, who had been so kind to them.

[44] The next Sabbath almost everyone in town came to hear the message about the Lord. [45] When the Jewish people saw the crowds, they were very jealous. They insulted Paul and spoke against everything he said.

There seem to be two groups of people who come to listen to Paul. One group is the Jews who are not happy about what Paul says. The others are not Jews. They are excited about what Paul says and want to know more.

Here's a 'brainbuster' question for you. You might need to ask an adult to help with the answer.

How can we know if a person is telling the truth about God?

(These may help!)

· Check what the Bible says.

· Talk with an adult who loves God.

· Ask your Sunday School teacher.

· Read your Bible lots and lots so you get to know what it says.

Sometimes when Christians tell the truth about God people will get angry and argue. The Bible says not to argue, but to speak gently and clearly. God can help us all to listen and understand. Sometimes people do not want to understand, and will not listen. Don't be one of those!

Prayer:
Dear God, help me to understand what you tell me in Your Word, the Bible.

58

Good News for the Gentiles

Let's look back on God's Mega Jigsaw Puzzle. What do you remember?

Abraham was given a special promise. God said that his family would grow and become a great nation.

Jonah learnt that God's love included people from other countries.

Peter discovered that God loves everybody, and that His plan is for all the people in the world.

Acts 13: 46- 47

46 But Paul and Barnabas bravely said:

We had to tell God's message to you before we told it to anyone else. But you rejected the message! This proves that you don't deserve eternal life. Now we are going to the Gentiles.
47 The Lord has given us this command,

"I have placed you here
as a light
for the Gentiles.
You are to take
the saving power of God
to people everywhere on earth."

Paul talked first to the Jews about God's special promise. Then he went to talk to people of other races.

Prayer:
Thank you God that you show your love to every person in the whole world.

Paul said (in verse 47)

**XYOUXAREXTOXTAKEXTHEXSAVINGX
POWERXOFXGODXTOXPEOPLEX
EVERYWHEREXONXEARTHX.**

Black out the X's and you will find what Paul said.

Paul on the run again

The Hotshots are packed and ready to return to base. They have visited lots of places where Paul went, but there are many more places still to go. Especially now...

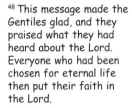

Paul was free to work with the Gentiles. They were ready to listen to God, and were full of praise for what God had done for them. They put their faith in Jesus, and the Holy Spirit came to them.

48 This message made the Gentiles glad, and they praised what they had heard about the Lord. Everyone who had been chosen for eternal life then put their faith in the Lord.

49 The message about the Lord spread all over that region. 50 But the Jewish leaders went to some of the important men in the town and to some respected women who were religious. They turned them against Paul and Barnabas and started making trouble for them. They even chased them out of that part of the country.

51 Paul and Barnabas shook the dust from that place off their feet and went on to the city of Iconium.

52 But the Lord's followers in Antioch were very happy and were filled with the Holy Spirit.

After Jesus returned to be with his Father, he sent the Holy Spirit to be with his friends. The Holy Spirit helped them to understand what God said, and to be strong in their faith. The Holy Spirit lives in us when we are a part of God's family. The Holy Spirit also helps us to listen to God.

Prayer idea: Think about the times you are glad that God is with you. Thank God for the Holy Spirit.

Miracles and wonders

60

The *Hotshots* have returned to base and are talking about their latest adventure.

> Paul was so brave to keep talking about Jesus when others were angry and hated him for it

One of the greatest miracles is that God changes people who believe and follow Jesus.

The Hotshots made a list of what Paul was like **before** he became a Christian. Can you think of anything else to add?

Make a list of Paul **after** he met Jesus.

Before	After
Determined	
Killer	
Traveller	
Jew	
Clever	

Wherever Paul went, people became Christians and new churches began. Some people were happy to learn about God and become part of God's family. Others would not listen and rejected the message. Each person alive today has the same choice.

Acts 14:1-4

Paul and Barnabas spoke in the Jewish meeting place in Iconium, just as they had done at Antioch, and many Jews and Gentiles put their faith in the Lord. ² But the Jews who did not have faith in him made the other Gentiles angry and turned them against the Lord's followers.

³ Paul and Barnabas stayed there for a while, having faith in the Lord and bravely speaking his message. The Lord gave them the power to work miracles and wonders, and he showed that their message about his great kindness was true.

⁴ The people of Iconium did not know what to think. Some of them believed the Jewish group, and others believed the apostles.

Prayer:
Dear God, Thank you for keeping your promise and sending us Jesus. Help us to learn more about Jesus and to become more like him.

ABOUT JESUS

This Hotshots book has been about Abraham, Jonah, Peter and Paul but the most important person in God's plan for the world is **Jesus**.

The Hotshots discover a lot about **Jesus** in some of their other adventures. If you haven't read them yet, here's some of the things they found out.

Jesus ...

was born more than 2000 years ago in Bethlehem, but he came from God.

When he grew up he told people about his father God and showed what God is like.

He healed people.

He hated unfairness and treated everyone fairly.

He loved everyone.

He showed his power over sickness and disease, evil spirits, the wind and clever people.

When powerful people tried to get rid of Jesus for saying he was God's Son, Jesus let them arrest and kill him.

It was all part of God's plan to pay for the wrong things we do.

God brought Jesus back to life and proved that all who put their faith in Jesus will live forever ...

just like Jesus.

Beginnin

The *Hotshots* have had great adventures meeting some of the people who were part of God's family long ago. These people were all very different. Some were young and some were old. Some were kind and some were not. Some listened to God and did what he told them. Some did not.

I like the way you don't have to be perfect to be part of God's family. It's not always easy to be a Christian.

Jesus gave us the Holy Spirit to help us be strong and know how to live God's way. We also have the Bible to learn about God and God's special plan for us.

We can talk to God any time wherever we are. God answers us in different ways, but we can be sure that God is always ready to listen to us.

ith GOD

Many times we may not understand what God is doing in our life. Abraham and Jonah did not always understand, but they still followed God.

God can see the 'big picture'. He knows how all the parts of our lives fit together – just like a big jigsaw puzzle. One day we will understand too.

Jesus wants us all to be part of His family. Here's how:

Say **THANK YOU** to God for loving you. Thank God for Jesus who came to show you the way to God.

Say **SORRY** for all the times you have not done what God wanted you to do. Ask God to forgive you.

Ask God to **PLEASE** give you a new beginning with Him. Ask Him to help you to listen and obey.

If you really mean what you say, you can be sure that God has heard you. You belong to God's family.

97

CERTIFICATE

Scripture Union
and
The

This is to certify that

....

....

(write your name neatly)

has completed the
stories and projects
from

God's
Mega
Jigsaw Puzzle

Signed: _Kate_ ....

Kate (Hotshots Leader)

Countersigned: ....

(Parent or other adult)

Date: ....